Addicted to Everything but Jesus

by

Ira Gilbert

DORRANCE PUBLISHING CO., INC.
PITTSBURGH, PENNSYLVANIA 15222

All scripture quotations have been taken from the authorized King James Version unless otherwise indicated.

All Rights Reserved
Copyright © 1999 by Ira Gilbert
No part of this book may be reproduced or transmitted in any form or by any means, electronic or mechanical, including photocopying, recording, or by any information storage and retrieval system without permission in writing from the publisher.

ISBN # 0-8059-4563-6
Printed in the United States of America

Second Printing

For information or to order additional books, please write:
Dorrance Publishing Co., Inc.
643 Smithfield Street
Pittsburgh, Pennsylvania 15222
U.S.A.
1-800-788-7654

Dedication

This book is dedicated to my father, Huey P. Gilbert, who passed away September 16, 1992. My father was a food addict, who was so heavily addicted that it cost him his life. He was fifty-seven years old and weighed six hundred pounds at the time of his death. He did not learn to control his eating habits until it was too late and health problems had taken their toll.

This book is also dedicated to my two daughters, Kamira and Angel, who inspired me to write it. They stood by me through the good times and the bad times. I love them both very much, and I truly give God all the glory for my daughters' strength and special understanding to help me overcome my addictive behavior. I could not have done it without their support.

Contents

Preface		vii
Acknowledgments		ix
Introduction		xi
Chapter One	My Story	1
Chapter Two	The Reality of Addiction	12
Chapter Three	Attitude	19
Chapter Four	Getting the Power	23
Chapter Five	The Purposeful Body	30
Chapter Six	Inner Healing	36
Chapter Seven	Temptations	41

Preface

God spoke to me about a year ago to write a book about deliverance and healing and to tell how God moved in my life. Let me explain. I was a young individual struggling with all kinds of addiction. I had strongholds in my life that could not be broken. I was addicted to everything but Jesus! I thought about suicide, but that was not the answer. I began to think, "How can I get out of all this bondage and be at peace?" I sincerely went to God because I had tried rehabilitation clinics and diet programs, and nothing seemed to work. I finally realized I could not do it myself nor with the help of others. I needed an inner healing and deliverance. I was so desperate that I would do anything to become free from these strongholds in my life. I began to seek God for my answer. I prayed, fasted, studied the Word of God, and started believing I could be healed, delivered, and set free!

Ps. 107:20 states that

> "He sent His word and healed them and delivered them from their destruction."

I now am totally free from any addictive behavior, and I give God all the glory. It was not easy because sometimes I still failed, but I got up and pressed on until I was totally free from any addictive stronghold in my life.

Satan's job is to keep you discouraged, defeated, and bound down with the cares of this world. As long as you have an addictive behavior, you cannot fulfill God's call in your life. It is not just enough to be saved. We must fulfill our purpose on this earth.

Acknowledgments

I would like to thank Jesus for giving me the strength to complete this book. I would like to thank the Holy Spirit for guiding me through this project, and I would like to thank God for bringing it to pass.

His strength has allowed me to step out of my comfort zone to fulfill my purpose on the earth.

To my pastor, Marvin Jennings, Sr., and my church family, Grace Emmanuel Baptist Church of Flint, Michigan, thank you for your love and support.

Thank you to Camilla Gilbert and Kimberly Creel for seeing the vision through with me.

To God be the glory.

Introduction

I am a former crack addict, food addict, and alcoholic, who started using drugs at the age of thirteen. I graduated from one drug to another. I loved the feeling of getting high and being the life of the party.

I was very popular and had many friends. I thought they loved me for me. In reality they only loved the drugs I could provide. All the while, Satan was trying to hinder me from fulfilling the purposes of God for my life.

Satan's stronghold on my life was crack. I wanted to commit suicide at times, but the Word of God, which was planted in me at a very young age, would leap up inside of me every time I considered it. I knew that if I committed suicide, I would be eternally damned. The guilt, fear, and condemnation that I was under were more than I could face. I remembered the words of Jesus:

> "Come unto me, all ye that labor and are heavy laden and I will give you rest. Take my yoke upon you, and learn of me; for I am meek and lowly in heart: and ye shall find rest unto your souls." (Matt. 11:28).

I am forty-one years old, and today I thank God because I am totally free and delivered. I have the ability to fulfill God's call in my life. I overcame several addictions.

Are you bound by an addiction? Do you truly want to be set free? Are you willing to earnestly pray, fast, and meditate on the Word of God? If the answer to each of these questions is yes, then this book will help you break free from all unholy addictions. You can be free, but freedom has a price. You can't hide your addictions any longer.

Chapter One
My Story

It is by the grace of God that I am able to share my story so that you may understand and have some insight into my life. I have hurt my loved ones and friends in my addiction. Most of all, I have hurt myself. I wanted to commit suicide daily in my addictions for more than twenty-five years of drugs, alcohol, adultery, gambling, and overeating. I was looking for love in all the wrong places. In less than one year, I had allowed the enemy to destroy my marriage, steal my family, put me in jail, and let me incur a drunk-driving charge. The result of the drunken driving charge was a year's probation and weekly urine test. I also was sentenced to an outpatient treatment center. If I failed to stay clean from drugs and alcohol, I would have to do jail time. This all happened when I was going through a divorce, and I was struggling with my addiction. The courts took over my life because of the wrong choices I made. I had no choice but to turn my life over to the care of God. I could no longer carry the pain, guilt, and embarrassment. I was a sick and defeated man. I did not want to live. I lost my family and the woman I truly loved. Everything was gone. I was broken, beaten, and humiliated.

My situation was like the one in this passage from the prophet Jeremiah:

> The word which came to Jeremiah from the Lord, saying,

> Arise and go down to the potter's house, and there I will cause thee to hear my words.
>
> Then I went down to the potter's house and, behold, he wrought a work on the wheels.
>
> And the vessel that he made of clay was marred in the hand of the potter: so he made it again another vessel, as seemed good to the potter to make it.
>
> Then the word of the Lord came to me, saying,
>
> O house of Israel, cannot I do with you as this potter? Saith the Lord. Behold, as the clay is in the potter's hand, so are ye in mine hand, O house of Israel.
>
> At what instant I shall speak concerning a nation, and concerning a kingdom, to pluck up,
>
>> And to pull down, and to destroy it;
>
> If that nation, against whom I have pronounced, turn from their evil, I will repent of the evil That I thought to do unto them." (Jer. 18:1-8)

I was ready for the potter's house. I had no one or nothing I could turn to. I looked up and said, "Lord, please help me." I was ready to be molded. My will had literally destroyed my life. I said, "Lord, not my will anymore, but thy will be done." My will had cost me everything but my physical body. My spirit was broken. I was sick, and I went into a state of depression. I did not want to live anymore. Sin had taken its toll on me. I was feeling like Job. The only difference was that I had brought it all on myself because of disobedience and pride.

The Bible tells us to love not the world nor the things in the world. Through it all, with the little faith I had, I cried out, "Lord, you have to help me." I pleaded. I begged. It seemed there was nothing I could do. I could not give it to the father I was serving. The only thing else he could do was to kill me. I had allowed the devil to control my will, emotions, spirit, and physical appearance. He zapped the life out of me. I had no other choice, if I chose to live, but to give it to God, and I did just that. He carried me until I was able to crawl, then walk.

The Bible tells us that when we are at our weakest, that is when we are strong. I could believe anything in the Word at that time. I was hurting. I would not want anyone to go through the hell I went through. When I hit my bottom, I was humbled through the things I lost and people I loved. I was truly all alone. God was the only one who could heal my heart and my wounds, and he did just that. To God be the glory. I am stronger today. I am encouraged, drug-free, healthy, and moving in the things of God that I might finally fulfill my calling on this earth. My purpose is to help this wounded, dying world. Just remember: with God all things are possible, and God has a way of getting your attention. Don't suffer like I did. You might not have the grace God gave me.

The devil wanted to finally kill me. He wanted me to be mad at God. I prayed and believed God would restore my marriage, and it did not happen. So, if you know Satan, he started working on my mind. He was saying, "You are doing all the right things—living holy, living without sin, living drug-free, and your prayers did not get answered." He tried to make me angry with God. I got angry with Satan instead because I recognized that Satan was the one that took me to the bottom. He is the true enemy of the cross. I just made up my mind that I might as well go through my problems, for they are only for a season. Allow God to heal the hurt, pain, and disappointment, and don't spend another day with Satan.

In the Book of Habakkuk, we read:

> "Although the fig tree shall not blossom, neither shall fruit be in the vines; the labor of the olive shall fail, and the fields shall yield no meat; the flock shall be cut off from the fold, and there shall be no herd in the stalls: Yet I will rejoice in the Lord, I will joy in the God of my salvation." (Hab. 3:17-18)

The love for God, like that of any devoted believer, is not based on what he expects God to give him. Even if God should send suffering and loss, his strongest manifestation of faith is in the Bible. Habakkuk declares he will still rejoice in the God of his salvation. I took that spirit and planted it in my spirit.

The amplified version of Hab. 3:17 says,

> "The Lord God is my strength, my personal bravery, and my invincible army; He makes my feet like hindsfeet and will make me to walk not to stand still in terror, but to walk and make spiritual progress upon my

high planes of trouble, suffering, or responsibility."

With all the hell I had been through, I had to start quoting the word of God to Satan and to myself:

"If God be for us, who can be against us?" (Rom. 8:31)

I had to ask myself to remember where I was. I thought I believed in God, but did I really? Why did all this happen to me? Sin!!

If I can weather the storms that have been in my life, nothing can separate me from the love of God, not even death. I am committed for life, because I really do believe that without God I would not have made it.

In Rom. 8:35, NIV, Paul writes:

"Who shall separate us from the love of Christ? Shall trouble or hardships or persecution, or famine, or nakedness, or danger or sword?"

And in Rom. 8:37-39, NIV, we read:

"For I am convinced that neither death nor life, neither angels nor demons, neither the present nor the future, nor any powers, neither height nor depth, nor anything else in all creation will be able to separate us from the love of God that is in Christ Jesus, our Lord."

RESTORATION PRAYER

I believe in miracles because I am a miracle. Old things have passed away, and all things have become new. I am washed in the blood of Jesus and freed from my addiction. Restoration and inner healing is my purpose now. If I am obedient to the Word of God, then I can do all things through Christ, who strengthens me. I am more than a conqueror through Jesus Christ, my Lord. I have surrendered all, and now I am totally free.

Any time you feel uneasy or feel addictive behavior coming on, keep saying this prayer. You need to memorize it, say it, and walk in it. You are a miracle. Your old, sinful nature cannot or will not manifest itself if you continue to leave the past buried. However, if you think about the old nature, doubt will manifest itself, and then unbelief. You have been healed and set free because Jesus paid the price on Calvary for your healing. Just keep on believing it, because when fear and condemnation rise up and you accept them, you have just put Christ on the cross. Walk in faith. Keep believing you are healed. Obey God's word and believe that you can do all things through Christ. Surrender all your weakness to him. You will be able to conquer any addictive behavior in your life. You will become totally free to walk in the things of God victoriously.

Remember

1) We are all restored.

2) We have received our inner healing.

3) We are obedient to the word of God.

4) We can do all things through Christ, who strengthens us.

5) We are more than conquerors.

6) We have surrendered all.

7) I am totally free.

The Works of Grace

I had been up for four days, snorting cocaine and drinking beer and wine. My body had become numb, and my senses were gone because I was so high. That day I went to pick up my unemployment check. I stood in line for forty-five minutes, snorting cocaine in the open. I even offered it to everyone, but I guess they were not as foolish as I was. I had white powder on my mouth and nose. My nose was running, and I was wiping it with my jacket sleeve while I was sweating profusely. I could have been arrested and thrown in jail or in a mental ward, but it was the grace of God that kept me from ending up in any of those ungodly places.

Once I took seven downers, not caring what happened to me. Later that night, I went to a dance, and my friends had to carry me out because I could not walk. I urinated all over myself. I went blind for a short period of time. They ended up inducing vomiting. If my friends had not done that, I could have died, but the Lord used them to show me His Grace.

Another time, I overdosed on crack after staying up three days. I thought I was dying. My chest felt like I had been hit by a diesel truck. The pain was unbelievable. I ran and jumped in the shower, but that didn't help. I stood outside on the patio. I walked around for about an hour, because I was to afraid to lie down or sit down. The fear was relentless. I knew I was going to bust hell wide open. I didn't go to the hospital because there wasn't anything they could do. My body had built up toxins, and I had to wait for them to clear from my system. Even though I knew I was dying, I still did not stop using drugs, but I did not die. That was truly the grace of God.

One day I had smoked up all my money. Then I loaned my car to someone, and I was just out roaming the streets of Flint about four o'clock in the morning. I was broke, miserable, and ashamed. I came to a bridge. The devil told me to jump, and I started to, but a small voice told me to choose life. If it had not been for the prayers of the saints and my upbringing, I would have ended my life. I just wanted the pain and suffering to stop, because it was more than I could bear. I knew suicide was wrong, but I knew I could not continue living like an animal. I even tried cutting my wrists with a knife, but that hurt too bad, and I just continued to lie in a tub of warm water. I took cigarettes and burned different parts of my body, hoping to get an infection, but it didn't work. I even played Russian roulette a few times. I only did this when I was using drugs. I just wanted to die. I could picture my death, and it was better than being found in a roach- and rat-infested crack house with no water or no sanitary conditions. Life had become deplorable. I had become what I feared the most—an animal, living for the next hit. So you can see, it was grace.

Once I was driving on the expressway about eighty miles per hour. Because I had been drinking and getting high all night, I fell asleep behind the wheel. The roads were icy, and the car went out of control and spun around twice. It was heading toward oncoming traffic. I ended up hitting the median, and that turned me back around. I eventually ended up in a ditch. If there had been any cars close by, I would have been dead. Someone could have hit me head-on. The only thing I lost was a muffler. I only lost that because the tow truck had to pull me out of the ditch. That was truly God's grace.

I was in and out of dope houses most of my life, but was never caught with drugs on me or in a raid. I remember three or four occasions when I left drug houses and then were raided by police three to five minutes later. It was grace.

One time I was stopped by the police and I had drugs in the car, but the officer let me go. This particular time, I was carrying two ounces on me. I was hiding them in the bottom of a snacks bag, just like I was coming from the grocery store. The police stopped me to search the vehicle. They let me go and told me to fix the tail light. I could still be in jail for the amount of drugs I was carrying, but it was the grace of God.

This book will build and strengthen your faith as well as change your attitude. It will prepare you for complete deliverance.

I went to a rehabilitation clinic for thirty days and started using alcohol again the day I was released. This time I was so drunk, I got into a fight and started to stab a young man with the first thing I found. It happened to be a barbecue fork for outdoor grills. I started to stab him in the chest. Surely I would have hurt him badly or even killed him, but something told me not to. It seems like I sobered up for a moment, and I eventually stabbed him in his leg. The fact that I did not hurt him any more seriously was truly the grace of God.

There were times when I would get so drunk that the devil would instruct me to take someone's life. I would become extremely violent when I was drunk. It would have been very easy to take someone's life. I didn't care. The drugs and alcohol were in control of me. I thank

God I did not kill anyone, because I wanted to on more than one occasion. It was God's grace that kept me from doing so.

When I weighed three hundred pounds, I looked like a stuffed pig. I was a very unhealthy walking corpse who was ready to have a stroke any day. All I did was eat, drink, and take drugs all day and night. I should be dead today with the way I abused my body and mind. I thought alcohol, food, and drugs could hide the pain and fear I was feeling. It's a wonder I have my right mind today. I thought I could find love in drugs and food. I was looking for love in all the wrong things. Christ is the only true love that understands our hurt and pain. It was truly grace.

Addiction is a bondage, but grace is love. Choose love. One year I was supposed to go to church on New Year's Eve, but I had to have one last party. I went and bought a quarter of an ounce of cocaine, and I had been drinking all day. Later than evening, I was caught speeding and got arrested for drunken driving. The police did not find the dope I had in the car, but if I had been in church, my license would not have been suspended, the cost of my car insurance would not have gone up, and I could have saved the money from the fines for drunken driving and the legal fees. Sin has a heavy price, but I thank God they did not find the drugs in my car. Some things will make you pray, and I was praying, "My Lord, don't let them find the drugs." It was truly the grace of God. To God be the glory.

In the gospel of Matthew, we read:

> "Then saith he unto his disciples, The harvest truly is plenteous, but the laborers are few; Pray ye therefore the Lord of the harvest, that He will send forth laborers into his harvest." (Matt. 9:37-38)

We the church always say to one another, "Lord, send forth laborers." Jesus gives us the key. He told us to pray that they be sent forth. Freedom is locked in prayer.

Elsewhere, Matthew also records these words of Jesus:

> "But I say unto you, Love your enemies, bless them that curse you, do good to them that hate you, and pray for them which despitefully use you, and persecute you." (Matt. 5:44)

These scriptures I have given you are a directive to pray for all of your circumstances. Unfortunately, instead of praying, you might want to murmur and complain. When you get mad, Satan attacks your spirit-man. He's got you right where he wants you—off balance. If you would only pray instead of using your emotions, then Satan could not use any stronghold against you.

Instead of arguing with your spouse, cursing at someone, and worrying about your bills, take it to God in prayer. Food, alcohol, and drugs are not your comforter. God is. Instead of manifesting the demon who seeks to destroy you, just manifest the fruits of the Holy Spirit. When you have not prayed without ceasing and you have not read the Bible, I guarantee that you will magnify the lust of the flesh—the sinful nature. This is why you are addicted to everything but Jesus.

Here are some other passages to keep in mind:

> This I say then, Walk in the spirit, and ye shall not fulfill the lust of the flesh.
>
> For the flesh lusteth against the Spirit, and the Spirit against the flesh: and these are contrary the one to the other: so that ye cannot do the things that ye would. (Gal. 5:16-17)
>
> . . .
>
> Beloved, think it not strange concerning the fiery trial which is to try you, as though some strange thing happened unto you.
>
> But rejoice inasmuch as ye are partakers of Christ's sufferings; that, when His glory shall be revealed, ye may be glad also with exceeding joy. (1 Pet. 4:12-13)
>
> . . .
>
> I returned, and saw under the sun, that the race is not to the swift, nor the battle to the strong, neither yet bread to the wise, nor yet riches to men of understanding, nor yet favor to men of skill; but time and chance happeneth to them all. (Eccl. 9:11)
>
> . . .
>
> And let us not be weary in well doing: for in due season we shall reap, if we faint not. (Gal. 6:9)
>
> . . .

Blessed is the man that walketh not in the counsel of the ungodly, nor standeth in the way of sinners, nor sitteth in the seat of the scornful.

But his delight is in the law of the Lord; and in his law doth he meditate day and night.

And he shall be like a tree planted by the rivers of water, that bringeth forth his fruit in his season; his leaf also shall not whither; and whatsoever he doeth shall prosper. (Ps. 1:1-3)

. . .

Beloved, I wish above all things that thou mayest prosper and be in health, even as thy soul prospereth. (3 John 1:2)

. . .

But the fearful, and unbelieving, and the abominable, and murderers, and whoremongers, and sorcerers, and idolaters, and all liars, shall have their part in the lake which burneth with fire and brimstone: which is the second death. (Rev. 21:8)

. . .

If my people, which are called by my name, shall humble themselves, and pray, and seek my face, and turn from their wicked ways; then will I hear from heaven, and will forgive their sin, and will heal their land. (2 Chron. 7:14)

. . .

Brethren, I count not myself to have apprehended: but this one thing I do, forgetting those things which are behind, and reaching forth unto those things which are before,

I press toward the mark for the prize of the high calling of God in Christ Jesus. (Phil. 3:13-14)

. . .

Blessed are they which are persecuted for righteousness' sake: for theirs is the kingdom of heaven.

Blessed are ye, when men shall revile you and persecute you, and shall say all manner of evil against you falsely, for my sake.

Rejoice, and be exceedingly glad: for great is your reward in heaven: for so persecuted they the prophets which were before you. (Matt. 5:10-12)

. . .

Persecuted, but not forsaken; cast down, but not destroyed. (2 Cor. 4:9)

. . .

To whom coming, as unto a living stone, disallowed indeed of men,

but chosen of God, and precious. (1 Pet. 2:4)

. . .

And said, If thou wilt diligently hearken to the voice of the Lord thy

God, and wilt do that which is right in His sight, and wilt give ear to His commandments, and keep all His statutes, I will put none of these diseases upon thee, which I have brought upon the Egyptians: for I am the Lord that healeth thee. (Ex. 15:26)

. . .

(To the chief Musician for the sons of Korah, a song upon Alamoth.) God is our refuge and strength, a very present help in trouble. (Ps. 46:1)

Chapter Two
The Reality of Addiction

Addiction is not a state of mind, but a reality. Let's set the record straight. People are addicted to more than just drugs and alcohol. A person can be addicted to cigarettes, shopping, food, and lust. You cannot allow an addiction to control you, because it will cause physical and emotional problems, which lead to death.

Crack is a demon sent from the pits of hell. It had complete control of me. It told me when to work, sleep, and spend my money—which was all of the time. It told me not to pay bills or buy groceries. I was instructed to pawn everything I owned and borrow money, even though I could not afford to pay it back.

At crack's command, I stopped being a father and a husband. I stopped being a man. I was dead inside. I had simply become a walking corpse, waiting for my flesh to die. But there is a God in heaven, and I have remembered his word:

> "Casting all your care upon him; for he careth for you." (1 Pet. 5:7)

At a crucial point in my life, I began to tire of the battle. I felt myself doubting God's word. It was at that time that I decided either this addictive spirit in me would be defeated or I would accept the fact that I could never be healed. I put a demand on God for my healing and, much to my surprise, He placed a demand on me.

God instructed me to seek His word, pray, fast, and believe. He said that Jesus had already paid the price for my healing and deliverance with His blood shed on Calvary. It was then that I changed my attitude. I quoted the word of God and walked in victory.

At times I stumbled and fell, but I simply got up again. I didn't have a pity party while on the ground, and I didn't allow guilt and condemnation to ride my back. Satan could not bind me with fear.

My attitude changed my beliefs, and my healing was manifested. The saints at my church knew of my problems—an addiction is never a secret—yet they never frowned on me. Those saints prayed for me, and they were an encouragement. They told me that

> "I can do all things through Christ, which strengtheneth me." (Phil. 4:13)

When I decided to surrender all to Jesus, that's when my addiction broke off of my life. Now it is your turn. Have you made the decision to surrender all?

Carnal Christians who are addicted are easily used and abused by Satan. The flesh reacts to problems. Drug users return to using, food lovers go back to eating, and whoremongers look for ungodly companionship. When you do this, you are doing exactly what Satan wants.

Until you change your reaction to circumstances and begin to pray diligently, Satan will use the same situations to keep you defeated, prayerless, and unholy. You cannot fulfill God's purpose for your life in this state.

Unfortunately, the church is sometimes seen as a bunch of failures who are unable to overcome our own problems. How can you help someone else get free from their addictions while you are still bound by yours? Our testimony is how we live and what people see in us. Unfortunately, most of us walk in defeat daily. If the Body of Christ cannot be delivered, then how can we help others become free? We live in a serious hour. Have you accepted your addictions? If you have, then you are backsliding, defeated, and a true enemy of the cross. Woe be unto you on judgment day.

No one wants to be addicted to anything. A person does not ask to be a junky or an alcoholic. These problems started out as an escape, a temporary solution that became a life-long problem. Hurtful situations wounded us and festered until prayer was not considered an option. It was then that fleshly resources—drugs, alcohol, eating, shopping—become our comforter.

Hiding the Problem

Why do you deny and hide your problems? The answers are simple: persecution, lack of acceptance, and fear.

The dictionary says persecution means to harass in a manner designed to injure, grieve, or afflict; to cause to suffer because of belief; or to annoy with persistent or urgent approaches. Someone with an addiction knows what it is like to be the object of persecution.

You don't want to admit that the opinion of others is important to you. Everyone wants to appear strong to other people. Society has a funny way of rejecting people when they have a problem unless they are rich or very popular. People do not want to admit they cannot overcome a problem, because we spend so much time looking down on them. In the Body of Christ, Christians tend to criticize rather than pray for that person who has AIDS or who is an addict. We tend to gossip instead of going to the people with problems and putting our arms around them and praying for them. We tend to run from and judge them according to their addiction.

It is really tough to be an addict. Most addicts stay in the closet because we, as Christians, are judgmental and not as loving as we ought to be. As a result, people can feel when others are talking negatively about them and when they are not wanted. If you had AIDS, how many people would you tell? How many alcoholics or addicts are still living in the closet? Are you one of them?

We can accept certain diseases such as diabetes and cancer, because these diseases are not perceived as being "bad" diseases. But a disease is a disease. The reason more people die with hidden addictions is because they fear being persecuted. It's time for the Body of Christ to grow up. How many skeletons do you have in your closet when it comes to addictions? Would your friends and family disown you because you are an addict?

The second factor that prompts you to deny your problems is lack of acceptance. You dread the lack of acceptance. Jesus said come to Him just like you are. Christ accepted each and every one of us in our worst conditions. He put only one stipulation on us:

> "If thou shalt confess with they mouth...and shalt believe in thine heart...thou shalt be saved." (Rom. 10:9).

Jesus accepted us unconditionally. Most of us say we want to be like Christ. Jesus loved the whores, tax collectors, and murderers, and accepted them and loved them if they would just believe. But we don't want to accept the whore, the wino, the addict, the murderer, or the thief. Yes, we talk a good game; that is why the world is yet dying.

Most people would rather deal with their addiction secretly than be around those like the Sadducees and Pharisees, because people can sense whether they are accepted or not. I guess that is why most pastors preach to the same people every Sunday morning. The wounded and hurting know that their way of escape will give them a conditional love for a season. I guess what I am trying to say is that people do not want the responsibility of accepting the problems of others. Yet we say we want to be more like Jesus. He loved and accepted everyone unconditionally. Do you love unconditionally?

Finally, fear or anxious concern also motivates you to hide your problems. Peer pressure affects adults. The desire to be with the "in" crowd remains long after high school ends. So many of us have lived with the fear of failure as well as success. We are afraid to come forth with our problems because we are not sure we can conquer them. But remember 2 Tim. 1:7,

> "For God hath not given us the spirit of fear; but of power and of love and of a sound mind."

If we would only just believe, because to fail or fall is not the end of the world. However, letting fear conquer us brings forth torment and condemnation. The devil has us defeated. When we give up, remember, he is already destined to everlasting fire and eternal damnation. He wants us to quit trying, and he wants us to live in fear of our addictions. If we do, Satan has accomplished what he set out to do, and that is to keep us in unbelief which breeds fear and doubt. In 1 John 4:18 it says,

> "There is no fear in love; but perfect love casteth out fear: because fear hath torment. He that feareth is not made perfect in love."

So we see that the opposite of fear is love and love can conquer all things. First we need to start loving ourselves again, to forgive ourselves for past failures, and to start over with a new purpose in mind that "we can do all things in Christ that strengthens us." We are not failures. We have just failed in our endeavors. Our thinking has been altered because of our problems. Prov. 24:16 says,

> "For a just man falleth seven times, and riseth up again: but the wicked shall fall into mischief."

We are human. We all have faults, some more severe and life-threatening than others. How many of us have lied to ourselves about areas in our lives that have us addicted—whether it is drugs, alcohol, food, lust, or gambling? On the surface, we appear strong and that nothing is hindering us from moving in the things of God. If that were so true, we would have more spiritual giants in the land. To struggle is not defeat, but to give up and continue to live in your addiction is sin.

Let's be honest. We were born into a world of sin. We have a sinful nature. Remember, we are only saved sinners by grace. Remember also that deliverance is an attitude. You are not a weak person to confess weakness in the flesh. The flesh is a weakness. It caters to everything but righteousness. That is why we must continue to deny the flesh. Finally, remember that you are not alone in your struggle to be free from addictive behavior. Prov. 28:13 says,

> "He that covereth his sin shall not prosper: but whosoever confesseth and forsaketh them shall have mercy."

So ask yourself, does peer pressure keep you from stepping out in faith and walking to the altar of grace or admitting you have a problem that the world might see? Are you as strong as you seem to be? Yes, I know you can take it to God in prayer in your prayer closet. That is exactly what the devil wants you to do—keep your addiction a secret. But when you openly confess weakness in your life, you are a marked person. Is it your desire to be with the "in" crowd, to be accepted by those you consider strong? Or do you desire to openly confess your weakness that God might show the power of deliverance through you and that someone else might receive his healing through your act of surrender? Publicly confessing your problem will allow you to let God move in your life. The acceptance of what people might think about you will not control your behavior. Will you allow God to be real in your life? God desires for all of us to be a testimony of power, of healing, and deliverance through Christ Jesus, our Lord.

Doubt

If you are hiding your problems, then you are afraid to face yourself. You probably are full of doubt, which means to fear, to suspect, to lack confidence in, to distrust, to be uncertain. This uncertainty often interferes with decision-making and gives rise to hesitation or suspense. It is an inclination not to believe or accept.

After all God had done to bring the children of Israel out of slavery, after all the miracles and the healing that were manifested, they still doubted God. They still mistrusted him and were unsure. Were they better off with God or the taskmaster's whip? They began to murmur and complain, like so many of us. God has blessed us with our life, health, and strength. He has blessed us to be prosperous and walk in the good of the land, but we still doubt his word.

Believe it or not, some people like suffering and complaining about conditions in their lives. Some just don't know how to receive their healing, and some just don't want to be healed. They choose to live in sin. First of all, we have to stop complaining and making excuses. Say to yourself, "I won't complain." Secondly, you might be in the wilderness like the children of Israel, but remember they chose to live in their situation because of murmuring and complaining. Also, it's time to believe that your wilderness is only for a season. Start seeing the promised land and believe God is able. You will start to rise above your problems and believe it is God's problem and not yours. He wants you to give it to Him.

I am reminded of a story in chapter thirteen of the Book of Numbers. After the Lord our God brought the children of Israel out of the wilderness, God promised them a land flowing with milk and honey. He had sent out the spies, one from every tribe, and it was just as God said—a land flowing with milk and honey. This is the fruit of it. God had already given them the land, but because of fear and unbelief in what they saw, the spies were frightened. All but two brought back this report. Num. 13:33 says,

> "And there we saw the giants, the sons of Anak, which came of the giants: and we were in our own sight as grasshoppers, and so we were in their sight."

What I am trying to say is that we have circumstances and situations that are giants in our lives, and we don't think we can overcome them because of fear and unbelief. But it was one spy who said, "Let us go up at once and possess the land because we are well able." We have to take on the spirit of Caleb in order to conquer the giants in our lives that are hindering us from walking in total victory in Christ Jesus. Remember, we are well able if we just believe.

Don't look at the problem, look at the problem solver, who has given us the tools to conquer giants in our lives. Quit looking at the giants. Stop saying, "I cannot conquer this problem." Quit listening to doubt and fear. Just start to believe, despite what you hear or see. Just believe you are well able. Remember that to live in fear and doubt is unbelief, and unbelief is sin.

An Excuse to Fail: Love Addiction

An addiction allows you to excuse your failures and enables the addiction to freely manifest itself at any time.

If you would just humble yourself, seek God, and turn from wickedness, you will allow God to heal your mind and change your heart. If you are addicted to anything that has a stronghold and can't be broken in your life, then you are hindering the move of God, not only in your life, but also in everyone else's life.

Fear, doubt, guilt, and condemnation are tools Satan uses to keep you from fulfilling God's purpose in your life. Change your heart, and your attitude will follow. Build your faith, and deliverance will come.

Chapter Three
Attitude

Webster's Dictionary defines attitude as "the state of mind, behavior, or conduct indicating one's feeling, opinion, or purpose."

Your attitude is the key to your deliverance. It unlocks the door to release your faith. Your change in attitude allows you to receive your healing. After all, as Gen. 18:14 says,

"Is any thing too hard for the Lord?"

You must believe that if God said it in his Word, then it is true, despite what you see, hear, or feel. The devil will tell you that deliverance is not for you. Satan is the father of lies. Every word that comes from his mouth is a lie. Don't you remember the first deception of mankind?

> And the Lord God commanded the man, saying, Of every tree of the garden thou mayest freely eat: but of the tree of the knowledge of good and evil, thou shalt not eat of it: for in the day that thou eatest thereof, thou shalt surely die." (Gen. 2:16-17)
>
> . . .
>
> And the serpent said unto the woman, Ye shall not surely die: for God doth know that in the day ye eat thereof, then your eyes shall be opened, and ye shall be as gods, knowing good and evil. (Gen. 3:4-5)

The devil's job is to bring doubt, discouragement, and fear to the hearts of God's people. If he succeeds, he has prevented us from accepting the truth of God's word. Adam and Eve failed in the Garden of Eden because they did not heed God's warning. They chose to believe the devil's lies rather than God's truth.

Satan is already condemned, but he wants to take every one he can with him into the eternal pit. It's his duty to discourage you from seeking deliverance from addiction. If you don't believe God's word and act on it, then you are just like Adam and Eve. God will drive you out from His presence because of doubt, fear, and unbelief.

Our attitude of indifference to accept our healing has allowed walls to build up in our spirit. A positive attitude reflects in our feelings, our emotions, and everyday living. We are who or what we think we are or believe ourselves to be. That's why the Word of God directs us to cleanse our thinking and to have the peace of mind that brings contentment. We need to think on pure and positive things. Phil. 4:8 says

> "Whatsoever things are true, whatsoever things are honest, whatsoever things are just, whatsoever things are pure, whatsoever things are lovely, whatsoever things are of good report; if there be any virtue and if there be any praise, think on these things."

Attitude is a reflection of your life in the mirror of life. It is how you react to your problem. It can continue to manifest itself and grow negatively, or you can stop feeding it and start believing that you are healed, delivered, and set free. Attitude will make you or break you. The choice is yours.

Faith

"Now faith is the substance of things hoped for, the evidence of things not seen." (Heb. 11:1)

Reach out and envision your healing and deliverance. You must see it in the spirit before it can manifest in the flesh. It is impossible to see yourself whole with your natural eyes. All that you can see is doubt, rejection, and failure.

You probably have visited the best drug treatment center, diet clinic, or financial advisor that money can buy, yet you still have your addiction. Why? The answer is simple. You are looking for deliverance in the wrong places. These places are good for a quick fix because the environment shuts out the world for a season. However, as soon as you come out of the center, the unchanged world is still here.

The same problems exist on your job, in your family, and in the community. You are no longer shielded. You are back in the real world. No one will monitor you. The temptation is always going to be there, so you can't run from it.

Webster defines diligent as "hard-working or pursued painstakingly." You must diligently seek God with all of your heart, mind, and soul. It is the working of your faith.

In Mark 5:25-34, the book of healing, it says:

> And a certain woman, which had an issue of blood twelve years—and had suffered many things of many physicians, and had spent all that she had, and was nothing bettered but rather grew worse,
>
> When she had heard of Jesus, came in the press behind, and touched his garment.
>
> For she said, If I may touch but his clothes, I shall be whole,
>
> And straightway the fountain of her blood was dried up; and she felt in her body that she was healed of the plague.
>
> And Jesus, immediately knowing in himself that virtue had gone out of him, turned him about in the press and said, Who touched my clothes?
>
> And his disciples said unto him Thou seest the multitude thronging thee and sayest thou, Who touched me?
>
> And he looked round about to see her that had done this thing.
>
> But the woman fearing and trembling, knowing what was done in her, came and fell down before Him and told Him the truth.

> And he said unto her, Daughter, thy faith hath made thee whole; go in peace, and be whole of thy plague.

You must have the same perspective of life as the woman with the issue of blood. She was tired of suffering and dirt poor from spending her life savings on physicians. When she heard about Jesus, she released her faith by changing her attitude. Notice I did not say that she took her problems to God before she met Jesus. She had to meet Jesus to be healed.

Just like you, this woman was looking for a man to remove her problems. Finally she came to the place of yielding and willingness to pay whatever the price in order to receive her deliverance. This was a woman of great faith.

An addiction is an "issue of blood" in your life. Build your faith, change your attitude, and touch the hem of His garment to be made whole. If you believed that you can be healed, then step out of your comfort zone and into faith. God can heal your heart and body but your attitude must change too. You must be ready to say, "Lord, whatever it takes I'm willing to surrender all."

People are dying and going to hell every day because they choose to live with their addictions. Look at the hundreds of people that you can help free once you are free.

Remember your faith in God is the key to your belief in receiving your healing. Your faith is the ability to believe, and how you believe is what you will receive. So remember 2 Cor. 5:7

> "For we walk by faith, not by sight."

and Rom. 1:17:

> "For therein is the righteousness of God revealed from faith to faith: as it is written. The just shall live by faith;"

and Hab. 2:4:

> "Behold, his soul which is lifted up is not upright in him; but the just shall by his faith."

Release your fears, let go of your doubt, and put your arms around faith. Your attitude and your belief will change. You can walk in total and complete victory.

Chapter Four
Getting the Power

"Now unto him that is able to do exceeding abundantly above all that we ask or think, according to the power that worketh in us. (Eph. 3:20).

How do you get the power to break free? It comes through prayer and fasting. You will never be delivered from any addiction until you deny yourself. Denial has a price, but it also contains an even greater reward. Forget about the old way that you prayed and fasted. Ask God to give you strength to begin a new course that will lead you into the fulfillment of His purpose for your life on the earth.

You must leave your comfort zone and place a demand on God for your deliverance. I could not break totally free from my addiction until I applied the principles of receiving spiritual power in my life.

Power Principles

1) Believe in the Word of God.

2) Pray like a man on a mission.

3) Fast and deny your flesh.

4) Attend church every time the doors open.

5) Lie on the altar, asking Jesus to have mercy on you.

6) Stay prostrate (lying face down) daily, until your spirit-man, though the direction of the Holy Spirit, begins to guide you into the healing process.

7) Memorize one scripture and repeat it daily.

The scripture that I kept before me daily during my healing process was Gen. 18:14:

> "Is any thing too hard for the Lord? At the time appointed, I will return unto thee, according to the time of life, and Sarah shall have a son."

By continually reciting that scripture and applying the power principles, I began to manifest the fruit of the spirit instead of the lust of the flesh.

Deliverance is only a sincere prayer away. Are you ready to be free?

The Power of Fasting

"How be it this kind goeth not out but by prayer and fasting." (Matt. 17:21)

Fasting is a command that most people don't believe or practice. Most Christians do not deny themselves. Fasting is almost a "forbidden" subject in the Body of Christ. We make excuses for not fasting, and then we wonder why our flesh continues to rise up uncontrollably. When you deny your flesh, you are sowing into your spirit.

To the Galatians, Paul writes:

> "Be not deceived; God is not mocked: for whatsoever a man soweth, that shall he also reap. For he that soweth to his flesh shall of the flesh reap corruption; but he that soweth to the Spirit shall of the Spirit reap life everlasting." (Gal. 6:7-8)

I am trying to build your faith so that you can walk into perfection and purpose on this earth. God is looking for willing vessels, holy and upright, without a spot or blemish to fulfill His purpose on the earth.

Jesus is the bridegroom who paid the price for the sins of the world. Fasting is meant for this present day and hour. The church as a body of believers would be stronger if there were more people denying themselves by fasting and praying that God's will be done.

Fasting opens your heart and tunes in your spiritual antenna. This gives you the power to overcome any addictive problem in your life. Deliverance is only a sincere prayer and fast away.

In Mark 11:24, we read:

> "Therefore I say unto you, What things soever ye desire, when ye pray, believe that ye receive them, and ye shall have them."

If you are truly bound and want to be free, then confess and be blessed, believe and receive.

In order to have a fasted life, you must have a spirit of humility. Fasting is a humbling process. It's a surrendering of the flesh and, believe me, your carnal nature will not have an open-door policy. The last thing that your flesh wants to do is submit. Your spirit-man will not be able to take control without a battle.

Your flesh will think of every excuse for not obeying. It will remind you every moment of the day that it is hungry. Your flesh will say, "It doesn't take all of this for your to kick the habit." Your flesh will quote scripture, manifest sickness, and even cry, but freedom has a price that you must pay. Deny yourself and subject your flesh to the Spirit.

Power Through Giving

Do not blame anyone but yourself for the financial disaster that you and Satan created together. Healing has a funny way of reminding you of your previous, conveniently forgotten bills. The world has not changed; you have—for the better. One consolation is that if you are paying bills, then you can see where your money is going—straight to the bill collector. It's okay, you're headed for financial freedom.

If you have sowed financial ruin, then you must reap the consequence of bad credit for a season. The length of your season is up to you. God will not perform a miracle in your finances overnight. If He does, then you just may forget where He brought you from and your previous state of mind.

It is not a punishment, so don't let the devil tell you, "If God is so good, then why are you in a worse condition than when you served me?" Just remind him that you are free and delivered from the chains of hell and that he is a liar. Remember, the deception in the Garden of Eden was the first big lie. Satan is using the same old tools and lies to fool you into believing that when you were with him, you were doing much better.

By allowing the Word of God to become your comforter and your guide, you have set yourself up to succeed. You cannot go wrong. It's time to get yourself out of debt. Give God ten percent of your income (tithe), and give offerings. The devil will attack you for giving, but give until it hurts. When you were addicted, you spent your entire paycheck serving that false god. Now you are delivered, healed, and set free, but you've decided to put God on a budget. Shame on you! You cannot tip God! You should ask, "How much do you want over and above my tithes and offerings?"

In 1 Cor. 4:20, we hear:

"For the kingdom of God is not in word, but in power."

Ask God to prepare your financial portfolio as you heal, and your finances will be restored. The devil will try to discourage you from giving, but remember everything is from God. Make the devil the liar that he is, and start walking in faith to see your finances restored.

This process of restoration may take time, but don't get discouraged, worried, and fretful. This is a good time to build your faith and watch it work in your life. No one can out-give God. You have victory now, but once your finances start to heal, purpose for your life becomes a clear vision, and you develop a positive cash flow, then you will have total victory over the enemy. It's then that you can really start walking like you are, an heir to the throne of God. When you receive your just inheritance, you will have a little Heaven right here, right now, on earth.

Money is power. Don't be afraid to step out on faith and take back everything that the devil has stolen from you—your health, finances, and purpose.

Prayer is a Treasure

"For where your treasure is, there will your heart be also." (Matt. 6:21)

Prayer should be just as important as eating in the life of a Christian. People eat a meal at least twice a day in order to sustain their mortal bodies. Some people even eat all day long. If you applied your eating habits to your prayer life, then you would be a spiritual giant. Prayer takes time and energy, but if you think about it, you take time for everything else. You spend so much time dressing, bathing, exercising, and showing off your earthly body that your spirit-man is starving to death before your eyes. No wonder you are addicted to everything but Jesus.

Where is your treasure? Is it in food, alcohol, drugs, cigarettes, credit cards, lust, or whoremongering?

Prayer is one of the most important tools you have in fighting the enemy. How can God speak to your heart when He can't get your attention? You are easily manipulated and defeated. All Satan must do is launch an attack against you, and you react exactly how he desires. He blows you off course every time.

Instead of praying about your circumstances, the attack triggers the addiction button. You find yourself searching through the refrigerator for leftover chocolate cake or headed to the mall for a shopping spree. You may even revert to alcohol or drugs. It's just a temporary fix to a permanent problem.

After you have stuffed yourself like a pig, charged the limit on your credit card, drunk yourself into oblivion, or gotten high, guess what? The problem is still there, staring you in the face. Prayer is the only thing that can change your misery. Any problem can be conquered if you would only believe that your prayers can be answered. Stop allowing Satan, the enemy of your soul, to trick you. He wants you to do everything except what the Bible says.

Take your burdens to God in prayer. Be spiritually minded, faith-believing, and prayed-up so that when problems arise, you can easily turn them over to God. Those who pray walk in victory every day. As Josh. 1:5 says,

> "There shall not any man be able to stand before thee all the days of thy life: as I was with Moses, so I will be with thee: I will not fail thee, nor forsake thee."

Or as we read in Ps. 37:25:

> "I have been young, and now am old; yet I have not seen the righteous forsaken, nor his seed begging bread."

Some people pray for only ten minutes a week and yet they want God to move mountains. Mountain-movers pray daily, all day long. People use all kinds of excuses for not praying. What is your excuse? A little prayer has no power, but lots of prayer yields lots of power. This is the power with which you can overcome any addiction. The devil only controls the weak, to keep them defeated.

> But thou, when thou prayest, enter into thy closet, and when thou has shut thy door, pray to thy Father which is in secret; and thy Father which seeth in secret shall reward thee openly.
>
> But when ye pray, use not vain repetitions, as the heathen do: For they think that they shall be heard for their much speaking.
>
> Be not ye therefore like unto them: for your Father knoweth what things ye have need of, before ye ask him.
>
> After this manner therefore pray ye: Our Father which art in Heaven, Hallowed be thy name.
>
> Thy kingdom come. Thy will be done in earth as it is in heaven.
>
> Give us this day our daily bread.
>
> And forgive us our debts, as we forgive our debtors.
>
> And lead us not into temptation, but deliver us from evil: For thine is the kingdom, and the power, and the glory, forever. Amen. (Matt. 6:6-13)

Find a prayer closet, a place where you can pray undisturbed and alone. Then follow the words of Jesus. This example of prayer is your guide, and it explains what we should pray:

1) that God's will may be done in our lives;

2) that God give us our daily bread—the Word of God;

3) that He might forgive us, as we forgive others; and

4) that He may help us overcome all temptations.

All it takes is a pure heart (pure motives), an understanding mind, and a willing vessel in order to receive your healing. Prayer is not an option but a must. It is not recreation but work.

Chapter Five
The Purposeful Body

"Remember them that are in bonds, as bound with them; and them which suffer adversity, as being yourselves also in the body." (Heb. 13:13)

It is important to attend a church that believes in deliverance and does not frown on people who have problems that can't be broken by themselves alone. We are part of a body, and just as the eyes need the feet to carry it toward what it sees, a person in trouble needs the Body of Christ to encourage him. The five-fold ministry gifts—apostles, prophets, teachers, evangelists, and pastors—encourage members to bring in the weak, broken-hearted, and those seeking deliverance.

Attack the devil with a warfare mentality and a warring spirit. Know in your heart and say with your mouth that God is a deliverer, a mighty man of war.

Go after the lost at any cost. God desires that the saints be unafraid to put their lives, time, and resources toward the saving of a soul. God wants to see his people saved, delivered, and totally set free so that the kingdom of God continues to be strengthened.

Unfortunately, people are afraid to ask the church for help because there are so many mean individuals in the Body of Christ. People with problems need to know they are loved. They can see through phony Christians and phony churches.

For centuries, Christians have hindered individuals through their language and actions from coming to Christ.

It is sad to say but sometimes there is more love in the world than there is in the church. Now is the time to see people as lost souls who are looking for care, comfort, and love.

We the church must grow up and accept our responsibility to our community, city, country, and world. The obligation to reach the lost at any cost is yours and mine. All some people want to know is that someone really cares and that love is free of charge.

As James 5:16 says,

> "Confess your faults one to another, and pray one for another, that ye may be healed. The effectual fervent prayer of a righteous man availeth much."

I can honestly say that my church is different. It is fulfilling its obligations and shouldering its responsibilities. I attend Grace Emmanuel Baptist Church in Flint, Michigan, where Marvin A. Jennings, Sr., is the pastor.

My former pastor began building my faith for deliverance from addictions. Pastor told me exactly what I had to do to be free, kept me attending church, taught me how to get into the spirit of praise and worship, educated me through ministry, and started me fasting and believing God. Heb. 13:17 tells us,

> "Obey them that have the rule over you, and submit yourselves: for they watch for your souls, as they must give account, that they may do it with joy, and not with grief: for that is unprofitable for you."

Pastor told me I needed a prayer covering, but most of all it was up to me. A prayer covering is a covering from the pulpit to the back door at church and at home. There are people who are sincerely concerned about your problems. They are put on guard to help shoulder the burden of prayer and discipline in your life until the addictive behavior has been broken. It keeps you busy with church work; it is a discipline in your life. It allows you to become responsible not only to yourself, but also to others. Ultimately, it centers you in the power of prayer. You are the focal point for these people until the behavior has been broken in your life. Most people who have addictive behavior do not have problems with rebellion, which feeds the addiction; so discipline is the opposite of rebellion.

My pastor provided me with the covering and the tools to receive my deliverance, but only I could make it happen. The saints from the church were praying for me, and I truly felt the love that people had for me and their desire to see me set free. The saints not only prayed for me but they also called and came by to visit. Sometimes I became upset because it seemed as though these people were treating me like a child, but now I understand why. My prayer covering was the Body of Christ.

Pastor and the entire church went out of their way to check on me. Pastor once said, "You have to make up your mind. Do you love God more than this addiction?" He was building my faith and supporting me even when I failed. Finally I saw, in the spirit, that I could be delivered.

I had to attack the root of the problem, because behind every addiction there is a different story. I found that I had to forgive the people who had hurt me. The deep wounds had to heal, and only God could do that. I obeyed the instructions of those who watched over my soul. A pastor's job is to guide and instruct you through the tough times as well as the good.

Connecting to the Body

"Therefore, if any man be in Christ, he is a new creature: old things are passed away; behold, all things are become new." (2 Cor. 5:17)

Pray about finding the right people who have the same interests you have. You want individuals who are not living in sin and who understand addictive behavior. They can help you stay on the Christian road of recovery. You need someone to talk with who understands the way you feel and the reasons why we confide in one another.

Let's get real. God places support in the Body of Christ. Sometimes you need someone cheering you on, telling you that you can conquer the addiction. You need someone who has battled with and overcome addiction, who is strong in the Lord and a living testimony. This person can help you adjust to your new lifestyle, encourage you to continue to seek God, and inspire you to stay prayerful. It is important to have a person or a group of people to talk with about these things.

It is important to be close to positive-thinking people for when the uneasy feelings, cravings, and desires begin to creep back into your life. You cannot ignore the warning signals. You can't afford to become slack because of the struggle, sacrifice, and hard work that it took to break the grip of the "strongman" from your life. Deliverance is a continuous process. Satan will do everything and anything to involve you with your old, sinful, addictive nature.

Don't worry about what other people will say; Jesus was persecuted and talked about. Jesus gave His life that we might become free from our addictions, worries, and problems. You will be lied to and your name will be destroyed, but who cares? Just hang on. This is not a game. If you allow the world to pull you back into your old, sinful nature, then you might not make it back. This may be your last chance. Heed this warning:

> "No man can serve two masters: for either he will hate the one, and love the other, or else he will hold to the one, and despise the other. Ye cannot serve God and mammon." (Matt. 6:24)

The choice is yours. Light cannot join in fellowship with darkness. They have nothing in common. Yes, your former friends will say, "You'll be back in a couple of months." You and I know that the devil is a liar, because if the Son shall make you free, you are free indeed. You must be strong, bold, and witty to take on the fiery darts of the enemy.

Consider these words from Paul's letter to the Ephesians:

> Wherefore take unto you the whole armor of God, that ye may be able to withstand in the evil day, and having done all, to stand.
>
> Stand therefore, having your loins girt about with truth, and having on the breastplate of righteousness.
>
> And your feet shod with the preparation of the gospel of peace;
>
> Above all, taking the shield of faith, wherewith ye shall be able to quench all the fiery darts of the wicked.
>
> And take the helmet of salvation, and the sword of the Spirit, which is the Word of God.
>
> Praying always with all prayer and supplication in the

Spirit, and watching thereunto with all perseverance and supplication for all saints." (Eph. 6:13-18)

Ephesians gives you all the tools you will ever need to stay an "overcomer." Don't drive around in the old neighborhood just because you think you're strong. The Bible says,

"Wherefore let him that thinketh he standeth take heed lest he fall." (1 Cor. 10:12).

You don't need to see old friends because old friends still have old habits.

I am not telling you this to run your life but to implore you to use wisdom in all you do. The life you save will be your own. If you can, change your environment. Move to a new location in the city. Change your telephone number. Am I telling you to run? Yes! I know this sounds drastic, but drastic times call for drastic measures. Do whatever it takes; your life depends on it.

A Brother is Born

"A friend loveth at all times, and a brother is born for adversity." (Prov. 17:17)

True friends are few and far between. I have a friend who took it upon himself to see me through my healing process. I am mentioning his name because he means a lot to me: Louis Junior. He is one of the kindest and most loving men I ever met. I call him dad, now that my natural father is deceased. This man has a genuine concern for me as a man and a friend.

When I fell, he was there to help me pick up the pieces. He called me three times a day until I was delivered just to ask how I was feeling and if I had any cravings. I could not get angry with him, although I wanted to, because he was concerned. On payday, the phone would be ringing as I walked through the door of my home. It was Brother Junior, encouraging me and even being stern with me when I needed it. He loved me, not as a junkie, but as a man full of potential and purpose waiting to burst through.

I love him for his part in the mending process that God started in my life. God sent a man to me who has become a true friend. To God be the glory!

We need more people like him in the Body of Christ—people

who have a willingness and drive to do whatever it takes to see you through. We want saints who are determined to see their brethren set free. Love is action, not words. Are you willing to help a dying world by showing just a little love? Freedom comes with a price. Are you willing to pay it?

Chapter Six
Inner Healing

"But He was wounded for our transgressions, He as bruised for our iniquities: the chastisement of our peace was upon Him; and with His stripes we are healed. (Isa. 53:5)

. . .

"He sent his word, and healed them and delivered them from their destructions." (Ps. 107:20)

To receive complete deliverance, you must have inner healing. Addictions are not surface problems; they are only reflected on the surface. Whether you are bound by food, drugs, alcohol, or lust, there is a rooted problem that developed long ago.

The root could be as deep as a dysfunctional family, a bad marriage, an abortion, an abusive parent, an incident of incest or rape. It can also be as simple as being blamed for something you did not cause. These hurts fester and become deep wounds. You know you have suffered a deep wound when the incident is in the past and yet you cannot get through it. You keep those feelings of rejection and hate. People with an addiction rise up and look for ways to vent their anger or frustration. They usually release it upon the addictive substance.

You cannot be delivered from your problems until you deal with the hurt, pain, rejection, and failure in your life that others have inflicted upon you. The loneliness and shame can be unbearable at times, which is why you can't get beyond the addiction.

Old wounds can continue to fester and keep you from fulfilling God's purpose in your life. No, it won't be easy, and the pain just won't go away, but you must learn to give it to Jesus. He wants your hurts, pain, and rejections. Jesus paid for all those things on Calvary. When you continue to bear the weight of them, you are nailing Christ back onto the cross. In 1 Pet. 5:7, we are reminded about

> "casting all your care upon Him; for He careth for you."

And Matt. 5:44 saying,

> "But I say unto you, Love your enemies, bless them that curse you, do good to them that hate you, and pray for them which despitefully use you and persecute you."

You must take the suffering to God in prayer. It is hard, but Christ is able to heal your hurts and pains. You must forgive those who injured you. You don't have any other choice in the matter.

Someone needs to hear your testimony. Do not become a hindrance to the move of God. Show that the devil is a liar by being healed, delivered, and set free. Someone else might become free through your testimony. Keep seeking God, stay prayerful, fast, and continue believing in God for your complete deliverance.

> "For we have not an high priest which cannot be touched with the feeling of our infirmities; but was in all points tempted like as we are, yet without sin. Let us therefore come boldly unto the throne of grace, that we may obtain mercy, and find grace to help in the time of need." (Heb. 4:15-16)

Also recall the worlds of Prov. 4:20-22:

> "My son, attend to my words, incline thine ear unto my sayings. Let them not depart from thine eyes; keep them in the midst of thine heart. For they are life unto those that find them, and health to all their flesh."

The Healing of Loved Ones

My ex-wife suffered more than I did. I thank God for a strong woman, because a weak one would have left me in the world to die. She continued to pray and seek God because she really loves me. She knew this addict was not the man she married. She recognized the spirit of addiction and the stronghold that had to be broken in my life.

An addict is a person who has been hurt. People are fragile. They are easily injured. Much of what you hear and experience controls your actions. If you would look inside an addict, the hurt would be apparent. Place yourself in his shoes; it will sensitize you. It's easy to say that an addict is weak. You're absolutely right, because human nature is weak.

Everyone wants to look strong, yet people are attempting suicide every day. People are afraid to face themselves because of what other people may think of their weaknesses and fears. No one wants an addict in their family, because it doesn't look good. We spend our time covering this addictive behavior, and it's our loved ones who suffer the most.

Your loved ones, spend so much time worrying that there is very little time for your physical and mental healing. You throw up your hands in defeat or tune the addict out of your life. Forget it. That will never work. You must deal with it. Why? Because they are related to you. In a family, what affects one affects the other.

We all have been touched by addictive behavior. We all have been hurt for years by someone we know who is struggling to become free. When you take a long look at the addict's problem, you find that you have one too. You have isolated yourself and your nerves are bad.

If you allow the addictive behavior of a loved one to control your life, then you are just as sick as the addict. In most cases, you are worse than the person with the addiction. You've asked the Lord, "Why me? I live right, pray, study, fast, believe in your Word, healing and miracles?" Ask yourself, am I manifesting the fruits of the Spirit?

Most loved ones who live with people or who are related to people who are addicted try to shield the problem. That is your first mistake. Don't lie. No one wants to have an addictive situation in their life, especially not a spouse or their children. No one wants to sit by the phone concerned that the next phone call will be from the police, telling you that your loved one is dead.

Addicted to Everything but Jesus

Sometimes you wish they were dead so that this whole thing would be over. If you could snap your fingers and everything would be all right, you would.

Don't allow the devil to convince you that if your loved one wanted to, he or she could change. That's a lie. Flesh has a mind of its own. It argues, fights, and creates bitterness. Your flesh will even tell you that you're not saved and your loved one will never be saved. Guilt, condemnation, and fear are what drives Satan. If a person is not walking in the light they are walking in the darkness and being driven by guilt, condemnation, and fear. Satan is the ruler of darkness.

Your attitude must change. Although it looks hopeless, just remember that God will not place on you more than you can bear. Recognize that you need deliverance too. A codependent is one who lives with an addict and takes on the characteristics and traits of the addict.

For instance, you worry, have insomnia, are moody, and feel like you want to die. An enabler is one who supports the habit with their finances or love. They pay all the bills, give the addict money to buy drugs or alcohol, and perhaps even bail them out of jail. They lie for them, make excuses for them, and often ignore the problem. If you want to see the addict delivered, then you must stop encouraging their addictions simply because they are someone you love. End the guilt trips.

In order for codependents and enablers to be delivered, you must

1) receive inner healing,
2) stop blaming God,
3) give a tough love, and
4) admit to God that you can't handle the situation and give it to Him.

God will deliver you from this situation. The person with the addiction may still have the problem, but you can receive healing for yourself. Instead of worrying yourself to death, give it to God. He wants you to cast all your cares on Him and not rely on your own understanding. Once you do that, begin to thank God for your healing every day. Instead of worrying, start praising God for your healing. The problem in the other person may get worse, but don't look to the natural realm; look into the spirit realm.

Satan will throw everything he can at you, but remain steadfast and unmovable. When you can't sleep, start praying and you will sleep. Quote the Word of God daily. Remember:

"Is any thing too hard for the Lord?" (Gen. 18:14)

Quote that to Satan every time he tries to bring a word of defeat to you. Remind him that he is already defeated and has no authority to speak in your life. Read 1 Corinthians, Chapter 13, every day until you feel your strength come. Manifest the fruits of Spirit. Then the problem will start bothering the person who is addicted. They will wonder how you sleep at night and why you are at peace. When they question you, tell them that you have turned them and their problem over to God.

"And let us not be weary in well doing; for in due season we shall reap, if we faint not." (Gal. 6:9)

Hold onto God's promises and a new strength will arise in you. It will break something in the spirit. You won't be bitter, angry, or vengeful. Tell the addict these things when he is sober, because he will not hear you if he is under the influence, and he may react violently.

You may have to leave him and move on with your life. This is where "tough love" comes in. God knows your heart, and that is all that counts. Someone else's addiction is not worth your losing your soul. It is not worth the worry, turmoil, stress, discomfort, and financial strain. It is time for you to heal and go on to fulfill God's purpose for your life in the earth.

Don't turn back on your loved ones, because only God can deliver and liberate. When the addict really wants help, he will seek deliverance by any means necessary.

Deliverance in any home starts with a change in attitude. Stop complaining and start praying. Stop fighting and start fasting. Stop falling and start rising. Are you ready to accept the change and rise to the challenge?

Chapter Seven
Temptations

"Finally, brethren, whatsoever things are true, whatsoever thins are honest...whatsoever things are lovely, whatsoever things are of good report; if there be any virtue, and if there be any praise, think on these things." (Phil. 4:8)

You need to memorize and recite this scripture constantly to keep those "good old days" stories buried. The problem is that you like to brag about how high you've been or how drunk you were. Those conversations stir up the old man, which is your sinful nature. When temptations arise—and you can rest assured they will—you must have on the whole armor of God in order to stand against the devil.

Satan will remind you of the good times you used to have while you served him. Let's be honest. There were some good times. However, let me also remind you that those good times are what brought you into your unsaved, self-destructive state. Satan's purpose is to catch you in your sin and then kill you there.

As long as you are alive, his mission is to kill you, steal from you, and destroy you. Whatever Satan brings against you cannot succeed unless you allow him to unlock the door to your pain, which you have buried and is in a dormant state. Remember, all sinful nature starts with the lust of the eyes, lust of the flesh, and the pride of life. Eph. 4:22-23 tells us:

> "That ye put off concerning the former conversation the old man, which is corrupt according to the deceitful lusts; And be renewed in the spirit of your mind."

And in 2 Pet. 2:4, we read:

> "The Lord knoweth how to deliver the godly out of temptations, and to reserve the unjust unto the day of judgment to be punished."

Understand that Satan is already defeated. It is you who gives him permission to come back into your life by becoming slack in your prayer life. You become prideful because you feel as if you've arrived. This is when Satan will send sinful thoughts through your mind. Remember, an idle mind is the devil's workshop.

Rebellion, Doubt, and Fear

"For rebellion is as the sin of witchcraft, and stubbornness is as iniquity and idolatry. Because thou hast rejected the word of the Lord, He hath also rejected thee from being king." (1 Sam 15:23).

Satan regains entrance into your life through murmuring and complaining. The next point of attack is your church attendance. Finally, you stop giving your time and resources.

If this is you, you are backsliding and a perfect target for the enemy to manifest the lustful spirit that leads you back into full-blown addiction. It might start with a beer, a joint, or a piece of cake. Before you know it, you're out of control and in trouble. Learn to recognize the warning signs. Don't play with Satan because he knows more tricks than you ever will.

You cannot allow the devil to force you into looking at anything from a carnal perspective. Remember, God has placed certain men and women in the Body of Christ for your perfection. When we rebel against God's shepherd (the pastor) we rebel against Christ Himself.

Heb. 13:17 reminds us:

> "Obey them that have the rule over you, and submit yourselves: for they watch for your souls, as they must give account, that they may do it with joy, and not with grief; for that is unprofitable for you."

When doubt creeps into your heart, it is time to strengthen your attack on Satan and put your flesh under guard.

Yes, you are to aggressively attack the devil. Don't wait until it is too late. Keep your oil burning daily with prayer and fasting. You have power to overcome.

Satan is already defeated. His greatest enemy is the Word of God. Use the Bible; it is your God-given resource. God's word is true. Just hold on until you receive your strength from heaven.

> "But ye shall receive power, after that the Holy Ghost is come upon you: and ye shall be witnesses unto me both in Jerusalem, and in all Judea, and in Samaria, and unto the uttermost part of the earth." (Acts 1:8)

The Transference of Spirits

> *"For we wrestle not against flesh and blood, but against principalities, against powers, against the rulers of the darkness of this world, against spiritual wickedness in high places." (Eph. 6:12)*

. . .

> *"Create in me a clean heart, O God; and renew a right spirit within me. Cast me not away from thy presence; and take not they holy spirit from me." (Ps. 51:10-11)*

Keep your spirit filled with the Word of God. You cannot allow your spirit-man to become stagnant. Webster defines stagnant as standing still, not flowing; and foul from standing. Your spirit-man feels and responds, just as your physical body does. The more you feed it, the larger it grows. Just as your flesh needs food to survive, so does your spirit. You are what you eat, naturally and spiritually.

If you hang around addicts, then eventually you might take on their spirit and become an addict. This is called a transference of spirits. Webster defines "transfer" as the ability to carry or cause to pass from one person to another. Monitor the people you spend your time with and the places you go. The transference of spirits is a real issue, but it is seldom addressed.

One day as I drove down the street, I saw two old friends walking. I offered them a ride; we only rode about four blocks. The thought of drinking or using drugs never even crossed my mind. I was fasting that day because it was a church night and my payday.

After dropping them off, I went home. By the time I pulled into the driveway, those spirits had jumped on me. I started manifesting my old nature and familiar, addictive behaviors. I started fussing about the house being dirty, and I began to clean. That spirit said, "Let's go party." I recognized something was drastically wrong, because I began feeling uneasy and jumpy. I was looking for an excuse to use. Finally I began quoting scriptures and singing praise and warfare songs to the Lord. I worshiped the Lord and cried out for His help.

The spirit of the Word said "pray." There was a war raging in the spirit realm. My flesh was battling my spirit-man. I got dressed for church and continued to pray. I was uneasy the entire day, but I achieved victory over Satan and my flesh because I did not fall into lust or temptation. I put on the whole armor of God and fought the devil with everything in me and won. I was able to discern the attack against my spirit-man. I didn't recognize what happened until I told my wife about the incident. The next day she sensed something was wrong and began praying. We figured out that their spirit had transferred to me as I gave them a ride. It is important to continually pray and study the Word of God that you may discern the works of the enemy.

The transference of spirits is real, so remember to use wisdom in all you do so that you may be able to stand victorious against the temptations and works of the enemy. The greatest attack upon God's children comes from within. You must discern whether a spirit is of God or of the devil. If you have your spiritual antennae up, and you are "prayed up", and you have the Word of God in your heart, then you can easily discern an attack. If you are not submitting to the Word and the Spirit behind the Word, which is Christ Jesus, then you will fall.

As Prov. 6:27 tells us:

> "Can a man take fire in his bosom, and his clothes not be burned?"

If there is any transference of a spirit into you, it should be the spirit of God only. It is not what enters you that defiles you but what manifests from your heart that is the source of your actions. You must be careful not to side with your flesh in sinful environments and sinful conversations. This includes going to church, your job, and your home. Satan won't attack you when you are prepared and on guard for him; he will wait until you least expect it or when you become overly confident in yourself. Think of what it took to bring you this far. It's going to take much more to keep you there.

Paul said,

> "And lest I should be exalted above measure through the abundance of the revelations, there was given to me a thorn in the flesh, the messenger of Satan to buffet me, lest I should be exalted above measure." (2 Cor. 12:7).

Christ told Paul,

> "My grace is sufficient for thee."

We don't know what the thorn was, but it caused Paul many problems. Your addiction is your thorn.

It's time for believers to take authority over addictive behavior in the Body of Christ. The only thing we should be addicted to is Jesus. We want to take the city, but we can't until we take the church.

Jesus said,

> "And these signs shall follow them that believe; in my name shall they cast out devils; they shall speak with new tongues; they shall take up serpents; and if they drink any deadly thing, it shall not hurt them; they shall lay hands on the sick, and they shall recover." (Mk. 16:17-18)

God's glory will not manifest itself until the church becomes healed, delivered, and set free. Fortunately, we have Christian therapists, treatment centers, diet centers, etc. Sometimes we have to reach outside of prayer so we know that we don't have to go it alone. I encourage people with problems to seek out people who are spiritual-minded and who deal with these problems on a daily basis in their secular jobs. These people could be sitting in your church congregation. You might not want to share your problems with just anyone. However, God might have placed such a person in the Body of Christ because He knows that we as humans need a human touch—someone to hold us, someone to cry on, someone to vent to, and who can deal with us from a Christian perspective. Sometimes we have to clean all the junk out before we can get to the root of the problem. If all we needed was prayer, Jesus would never have made the statement

"They that are whole need not a physician, but they that are sick." (Lk. 5:31).

We all need someone we can trust and talk to in times of crisis or good times. Remember, you don't have to go it alone. You can always reach out and ask for help. Pray about it. Allow the Lord to lead you to that center or individual. Loneliness is a spirit of rejection, hurt, and pain that brings negative thoughts and feelings of unworthiness, insecurity, and pain.

God's Healing and Restoration

God's desire is that we be free from our addictive behavior, that we no longer carry condemnation and fear and continue to walk in unbelief. God's desire is that we become healed, delivered, and set free, that we might fulfill the call of God in our life. Everyone has a purpose on earth and is charged by God to bring it to fulfillment. How many souls have died and gone to hell because they didn't fulfill their calling? It's high time we receive our healing so we can have a little heaven on earth. Peace be unto you, and remember, there is nothing too hard for God.

I can truly thank God for victory. I have been drug-free for almost five years. Some people will say it's not long, but if you have traveled down the roads I have gone, you would give God all the glory. I know healing is a continuous process. For by His stripes I am healed.

God gave me something that no man can take away, and that is a new life and a new beginning. I am taking back everything the devil stole from me. I remarried my first wife and only love. I took back my marriage and my family. I am taking back my finances, my destiny, and my purpose.

Who we are who we are destined to become is up to us. God has provided the tools. We already have the victory. We have to pour our heart, mind, and soul into the truth so that our spirit-man can be revived, renewed, and restored to bring forth godly perfection that will usher us into what god has called us to do. Not facing the truth forbids us from being healed, delivered, and totally free. The truth which is God's Word can only abide in harmony together with His Spirit.

To God be the glory!